D is for DAVID

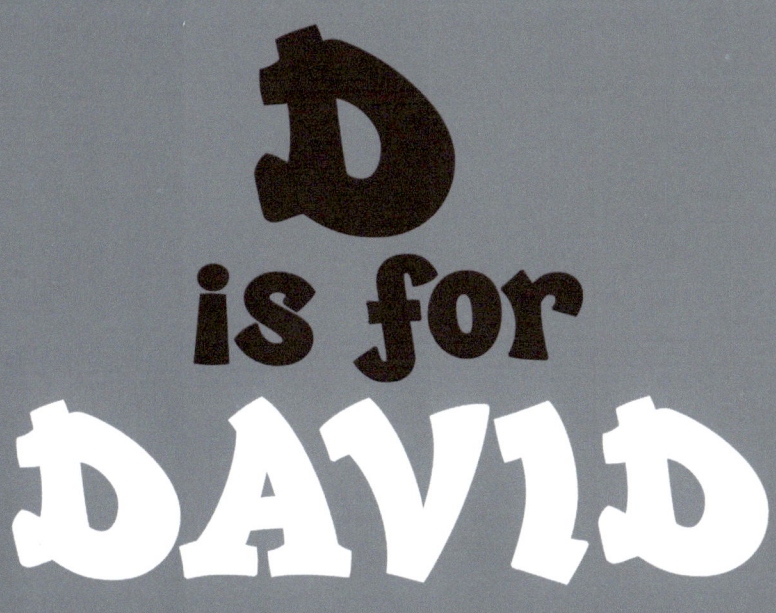

Dr. C. White-Elliott

Illustrated by Megan Hyson

www.clfpublishing.org
909.315.3161

Copyright © 2020 by Cassundra White-Elliott

All rights reserved. No portion of this book may be reproduced, stored in a retrieval system, or transmitted by any form or any means electronically, photocopied, recorded, or any other except for brief quotations in printed reviews, without the prior permission of the publisher.

Illustrations by Megan Hyson.

Contact Info: mhyson@salutationsstjohn.com   www.salutationstjohn.com

ISBN # 978-1-945102-48-6

Printed in the United States of America.

For
Kayden Hunter
my granddaughter

King David was the second and most popular king of Israel. He was a man who really loved God and wanted to please God in all that he did. He wasn't perfect, but he always tried to make things right.

But, David wasn't always a king. Before David became king, he was responsible for taking care of the family sheep. One day, a lion was trying to attack the sheep. David had no choice but to kill the lion to save the sheep.

Later, David had to save the sheep again. That time, he came up against a bear. But, David was brave. Like with the lion, David had to kill the bear because it tried to carry one of the sheep away.

When David was a little older, his people (the Israelites) went to war against the Philistines. Goliath, one of the Philistine warriors, was over 9-feet tall. He was considered a giant. Goliath told the Israelites to send a man to fight one-on-one against him.

When David heard Goliath's request, he told King Saul he was willing to go up against Goliath. David was willing to fight to save his people.

Finally, King Saul agreed to allow David to fight Goliath. So, David took a slingshot and five stones to battle with him against Goliath. Who do you think will win?

David defeated Goliath in battle by hitting him in the head, by using the slingshot and only one of the five stones.

Just like you may have brothers and sisters. David had seven brothers, but he also had a best friend whose name was Jonathan. Jonathan was King Saul's son.

Sometime later, when David was a little older, King Saul was killed. Then, it was time for David to take the throne, becoming the second king for all of Israel.

Later, King David married Bathsheba. They had a son named Solomon, who would eventually become the next king.

King David was a great king.
He loved God, and God let him be
king over Israel for 40 years.

www.ingramcontent.com/pod-product-compliance
Lightning Source LLC
Chambersburg PA
CBHW041933160426
42813CB00103B/2915